TIDE POOLS

By Melissa Cole
Photographs By Brandon Cole

BLACKBIRCH®
PRESS

THOMSON
✳
GALE

San Diego • Detroit • New York • San Francisco • Cleveland • New Haven, Conn. • Waterville, Maine • London • Munich

For more information, contact
The Gale Group, Inc.
27500 Drake Rd.
Farmington Hills, MI 48331-3535
Or you can visit our Internet site at http://www.gale.com

Photo Credits: Cover, all photos © Brandon D. Cole; illustrations by Chris Jouan Illustration

LIBRARY OF CONGRESS CATALOGING-IN-PUBLICATION DATA

Cole, Melissa
 Tide pools / by Melissa Cole.
    p. cm. — (Wild marine habitats)
Includes bibliographical references
Contents: Where are tide pools found today? — Plants — Animals — Food chain.
  ISBN 1-56711-912-3 (hardback : alk. paper)
  1. Tide pool ecology—Juvenile literature. [1. Tide pool ecology. 2. Tide pools. 3. Ecology.] I. Title.

  QH541.5.S35C653 2004
  551.46—dc22

                                                        2003019616

Printed in the United States
10 9 8 7 6 5 4 3 2 1

Contents

Introduction

A habitat is a place where certain animals and plants live together naturally. There are many different types of ocean habitats. One of these habitats is a tide pool. Tide pool habitats are found on rocky ocean shores.

Twice a day, during the high tide, waves wash over the coastline and splash up on the shore. As the tide recedes, water is left behind in the rocky areas from the shore out to the water's edge. These pools of water are known as tide pools. Some tide pools are small, shallow puddles, and some are as big as swimming pools.

Many plants and animals make their homes in the tide pools of rocky ocean shores.

Where Are Tide Pools Found Today?

Tide pools are found worldwide, wherever ocean waves wash up on rocky shores. They are common off the Pacific coast of North America, from Alaska to Mexico's northern Baja peninsula. Tide pools are found along both sides of the North and South Atlantic, including the coasts of the northeastern United States, Great Britain, and Chile.

There are tide pools in rocky shores of the Pacific Northwest (inset) all the way down to the warmer waters of Mexico's Baja peninsula.

There are also tide pools in tropical areas such as Hawaii and Australia. They are also found along the rocky volcanic shores of Japan and the Galapagos Islands.

Tide pools have formed in the volcanic rock of the Galapagos Islands' shoreline.

Tide pools are difficult habitats for animals to live in because the pools constantly change with the tides. During high tides, waves bring water, oxygen, food particles, and floating seaweed to tide pools. During low tides, however, waves often do not reach the tide pools on shore. As these pools warm up in the sun, they lose water through evaporation. Salt from the ocean water is left behind. This can make the tide pools too salty for the animals that live in them. Some tide pools even dry up completely. This exposes their inhabitants to the wind and sun until the next high tide brings more water to the pool.

High tides (inset) bring water, oxygen, and food to tide pools.

Sometimes at low tide, waves cannot reach the tide pools and the pools may dry up.

Climate

Tide pools are found in many different areas around the world. As a result, their climates vary. Tide pools are found in cool, windy places like the shore of Maine. They are also found in warm, tropical places like Hawaii. Tropical tide pool animals include small fish, crabs, sea urchins, shrimp, and octopuses. Cool-water tide pools are home to a larger variety of animals, such as starfish, anemones, clams, and mussels. They can also contain barnacles, sea urchins, fish, and crabs.

The coasts of New England and western North America are often foggy in the summer. Fog provides moisture for tide pool plants and animals. It also protects them from the sun's heat when they are not covered with water.

Topography

Scientists divide the tide pool habitat into three main zones. Different plants and animals have adapted to each tide pool zone. This is known as zonation. The subtidal zone is the area closest to the ocean. It is often completely covered with water, but not always. During very low tides, it has tide pools. The area between the high-tide and low-tide marks is known as the intertidal zone. It is the widest of the three areas. The intertidal zone has more tide pools than the other two zones because it is covered and uncovered twice a day by the incoming and outgoing tides. The splash zone is the area above the high tide mark. It only has tide pools when splashed by waves or during very high tides.

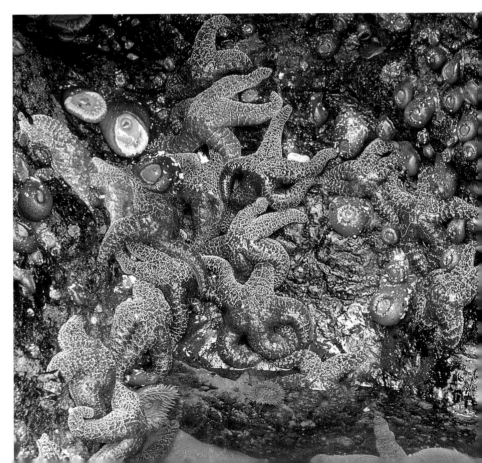

Opposite and right: Starfish are among the large variety of animals that live in cool-water tide pools. At very low tides, tide pool animals are exposed.

Many types of plants live in tide pools. Some plants, such as palm kelp, have rootlike structures called holdfasts. Holdfasts firmly attach the plants to rocks. Tiny plants called phytoplankton float freely in ocean water. They wash in with the tides and provide food for tide pool animals. Surfgrass is plentiful in many tide pools. It is a flowering plant similar to a water lily.

Seaweed is another type of plant found in tide pools. It belongs to a group of plants called algae. There are three main types of seaweed: green, brown and red. Green algae such as sea lettuce often grows in shallow tide pools found high up on shore.

Kelp, seaweed, and other types of algae (inset) grow in tide pools.

Brown algae, including kelp and bladder wrack, grows in pools farther down shore in the intertidal zone. Red algae grows in subtidal pools closest to the ocean. The red color of this seaweed helps it to absorb sunlight even in deep pools where very little light reaches below the surface. Green and brown algae can only absorb sunlight in shallow water.

Animals

As high tides wash up onto the shore, they carry a wide variety of sea creatures with them. Small crabs, starfish, and fish are tossed into tide pools by the waves. Many of these animals spend the rest of their lives in a single tide pool. Others swim in and out with the tides.

Predators are animals that hunt and eat other animals. Many land predators that are not tide pool residents come to the pools in search of food. For example, bears often visit tide pools from nearby forests in search of small fish and crabs. Raccoons and mink also depend on tide pools for food. They skillfully use their paws to scoop mussels, clams, fish, and shrimp from the water. Many

The oystercatcher (pictured) and other seabirds feed on tide pool animals.

types of seabirds, such as seagulls, sandpipers, and oystercatchers, prey on tide pool animals.

Within the tide pools other predators can be found. Small octopuses crawl from pool to pool on their suction-cupped tentacles. Crabs are their favorite prey. Sculpins are small fish that are often the same color as their surroundings. This camouflage allows these tide pool hunters to sneak up on prey such as small shrimp and fish. Starfish are common tide pool predators. They use their strong grip to pry open mussels and clams.

Octopuses (above) capture prey with their tentacles while sculpins (below) use camouflage to sneak up on smaller animals.

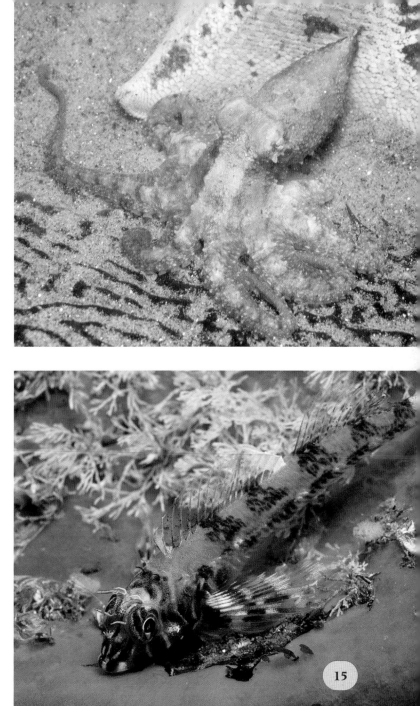

Many shelled animals make tide pools their home. Sea snails, such as periwinkles, limpets, and chitons, often cluster together on tide pool rocks. They feed on phytoplankton and seaweed. All sea snails use their radula, or tongue, to scrape algae off rocks as they crawl along. Sea urchins feed on algae and seaweed, too. Their bodies are covered with sharp, poisonous spines that protect them from most predators.

Some tide pool animals, such as clams and mussels, strain tiny food particles and phytoplankton from the water. They are known as filter feeders. Mussels begin life as tiny swimming larvae. The larvae settle on rocks. Then they send out small streams of fluid that harden to become tough, flexible threads. The mussels use these extremely strong threads to attach themselves to the rocks. This keeps them from being tumbled about in the surf. Then they begin to extract minerals from the water to form their shells.

Opposite: Some tide pool rocks are covered with mussels and barnacles.
Inset: Sea urchins and starfish cluster on other rocks.

Barnacles, which are related to crabs, are another type of filter feeder. They produce a cementlike substance to permanently attach themselves to rocks, wood, and even the shells of other animals.

Their six pairs of feathery legs stick out of their dome-shaped shells and sweep plankton toward their mouths.

Sea anemones look like flowers, but they are actually filter-feeding animals as well. A ring of stinging tentacles surrounds their mouths. These tentacles paralyze and grab plankton, shrimp, and sometimes even small fish.

Tide pools are kept clean by a group of animals called scavengers. Scavengers feed on dead plants and animals that wash into the pools with the tide. Seagulls, sea cucumbers, brittle stars, hermit crabs, and shrimp are examples of tide pool scavengers.

Below: Sea anemones use the stinging tentacles around their mouth to capture prey.
Opposite: Some crabs are scavengers that eat dead animals that wash into tide pools.

Many tide pool animals store water in their tissues so they will not dry up in the sun. For example, limpets, a type of snail with a dome-shaped shell, use a round, muscular organ called a foot to stick to rocks. They tightly clamp down against the rocks to form a seal. This keeps them from losing moisture when they are out of water. Anemones store water in their bodies and keep their tentacles tucked inside when their pools dry up. Other animals, such as crabs, hide beneath clumps of damp seaweed to stay wet.

Food Chain

All living things need to feed or gain energy to live. In a tide pool, seaweed absorbs sunlight to make energy. When a sea snail such as a limpet eats the seaweed, some of the plant's energy becomes part of the snail. When the snail is eaten by a crab, which in turn is eaten by a sculpin, the energy is passed from creature to creature. If the sculpin dies and sinks to the bottom of the tide pool, scavengers such as starfish and hermit crabs feed on the remains and gain energy for themselves. Decomposers such as worms and bacteria break down the last bits. Any leftovers mix with the water. Seaweed absorbs these nutrients from the water in addition to the energy that it receives from the sun. Then the whole cycle begins again.

This process of energy passing between organisms is called a food chain. Several food chains linked together are called a food web. Ecologists use food web diagrams to show the relationship between organisms that live together in a habitat community.

In a tide pool food chain, energy is passed from the sun to plants and then from creature to creature.

A Tide Pool's Food Chain

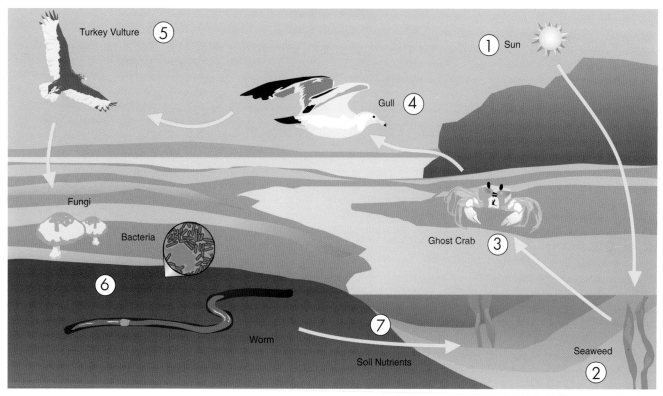

The food chain shows a step-by-step example of how energy in the tide pool habitat is exchanged through food: (1) sunlight is used by (2) seaweed to make sugar, which is then stored in its fronds. When a (3) ghost crab eats the seaweed, some of the plant's energy becomes part of the crab. When a (4) seagull eats a ghost crab, the energy is passed from creature to creature. When the gull dies, scavengers such as (5) turkey vultures and beach hoppers feed on the waste. Decomposers such as (6) bacteria and worms break down the last bits and become part of the sand or mix with the seawater. Seaweed absorbs these (7) nutrients directly from water in addition to the energy that their fronds receive from the sun. Then the whole cycle begins again.

Humans and Tide Pools

Tide pools are easily damaged by pollution because they are found on shore. They are often close to towns and factories. When it rains, pollutants from factories, household chemicals, and sewage leaks can wash into tide pools and kill the animals that live there. Trash such as broken fishing lines, plastic bottles, and ropes are brought in by the tides. This litter can entangle and injure tide pool animals. Oil spills are also very harmful to tide pool animals and sea birds.

People sometimes collect animals such as snails, sea stars, and fish from tide pools to use for food and tourist souvenirs. This can decrease the populations of certain animals. It can also disrupt the balance of creatures within the tide pools. In many places, such as Cape Perpetua on the Oregon coast, tide pool habitats have been set aside as protected parks. In these areas, people are not allowed to take tide pool creatures. Protection of these tide pool areas should ensure that tide pool habitats remain healthy for many years to come.

When people collect tide pool animals as souvenirs, they disrupt the habitat's delicate balance.

A Tide Pool's Food Web

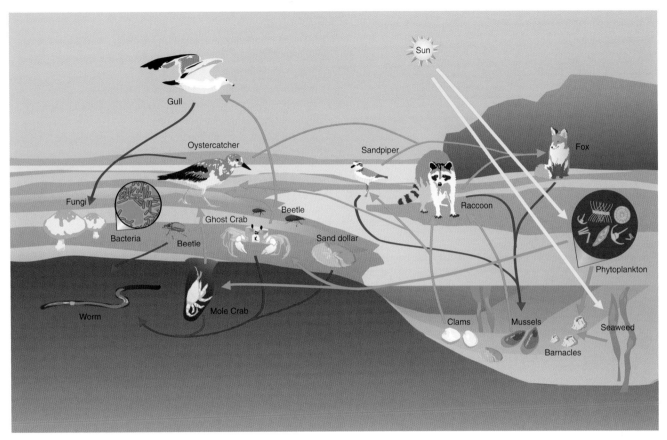

Food webs show how creatures in a habitat depend on one another to survive. The arrows in this drawing show the flow of energy from one creature to another. Yellow arrows: green plants that make food from air and sunlight; Green arrows: animals that eat the green plants; Orange arrows: predators; Red arrows: scavengers and decomposers. These reduce dead bodies to their basic chemicals, which return to the soil to be taken up by green plants, beginning the cycle all over again.

Glossary

Algae Simple plants that do not produce roots or flowers; seaweeds are algae

Camouflage A coloration or shape that allows a plant or animal to be hidden in its environment

Decomposers Animals such as worms and bacteria that eat dead tissue and return nutrients to the water

Habitat The area in which a plant or animal naturally lives. A habitat provides living organisms with everything they need to survive— food, water, and shelter.

Holdfast A rootlike structure that holds some seaweed to hard surfaces like rocks

Oxygen A colorless, odorless gas that animals need to breathe

Predators Animals such as octopuses, that hunt other animals for their food

Prey An animal hunted by another animal

Radula The rough tongue of a snail used to scrape algae off of rocks or bore through shells of prey

Scavengers Animals such as starfish that feed on animals that are already dead

For More Information

Books

Bredeson, Carmen. *Tide Pools.* Danbury, CT: Grolier Publishing, 1999.
Cohat, Elizabeth. *The Seashore.* New York: Scholastic, 1995.
McLeish, Ewan. *Habitats: Oceans and Seas.* Austin, TX: Steck-Vaughn, 1997.

Web Site

Explore a virtual tidepool at
www.pbs.org/wnet/nature/edgeofsea/tidepool.html

Index